Easy Caramel Cookbook

50 Delicious Caramel Recipes

By
BookSumo Press
Copyright © by Saxonberg Associates
All rights reserved

Published by
BookSumo Press, a DBA of Saxonberg Associates
http://www.booksumo.com/

ABOUT THE AUTHOR.

BookSumo Press is a publisher of unique, easy, and healthy cookbooks.

Our cookbooks span all topics and all subjects. If you want a deep dive into the possibilities of cooking with any type of ingredient. Then BookSumo Press is your go to place for robust yet simple and delicious cookbooks and recipes. Whether you are looking for great tasting pressure cooker recipes or authentic ethic and cultural food. BookSumo Press has a delicious and easy cookbook for you.

With simple ingredients, and even simpler step-by-step instructions BookSumo cookbooks get everyone in the kitchen chefing delicious meals.

BookSumo is an independent publisher of books operating in the beautiful Garden State (NJ) and our team of chefs and kitchen experts are here to teach, eat, and be merry!

INTRODUCTION

Welcome to *The Effortless Chef Series*! Thank you for taking the time to purchase this cookbook.

Come take a journey into the delights of easy cooking. The point of this cookbook and all BookSumo Press cookbooks is to exemplify the effortless nature of cooking simply.

In this book we focus on Caramel. You will find that even though the recipes are simple, the taste of the dishes are quite amazing.

So will you take an adventure in simple cooking? If the answer is yes please consult the table of contents to find the dishes you are most interested in.

Once you are ready, jump right in and start cooking.

— BookSumo Press

TABLE OF CONTENTS

About the Author 2

Introduction 3

Table of Contents 4

Any Issues? Contact Us 7

Legal Notes 8

Common Abbreviations 9

Chapter 1: Easy Caramel Recipes 10

    Opera Playhouse Popcorn 10

    Crusty Caramel Crisps 13

    Autumn Pastry 16

    Lunch Box Oat Squares 19

    Caramel Bars 22

    Aunty Pari's Brownies 25

    Caramel Coffee Candies 28

    Caramel Chops 31

    3-Ingredient Patty Pie 34

    A 3rd Grader's Lunch Box Snack 36

Arabian Dream Grapes 39

London Street Cookies 41

4-Ingredient Dessert Glaze 44

3-Ingredient Apples 46

Scottish Bread 48

Caramel Country Bars 51

1-Ingredient Caramel Sauce 54

Valentine's Day Truffle's 56

Cream Cheese Caramel Candy 58

Pre-Colonial Candy 61

Winter Carnival Popcorn 64

Margarita's Flan 66

Asian Fusion Sweet Chicken 69

Manhattan Bridge Cheesecake 72

Caramel Cream Dream 75

Sunday's Breakfast 78

Caramel Coocoo's 81

Macho Macchiato 83

Picnic Fudge 85

How to Make a Caramel Roll 89

Central American Inspired Flan 93

A Simple Cake Topping.. 96

Canadian Country Apple Crisp 98

State Fair Apples... 100

Catalina's Crazy Custard 103

Deluxe French Toast 101.. 106

Lover's Movie-Time Popcorn... 109

Nutty Cake from Munich 111

Simple Life Grapes.. 113

Cream Cheese Parfait... 115

Caramel Parfait 118

Vanilla Caramel Bars 121

Walnuts and Caramel 124

Warm Spiced Popcorn 126

THANKS FOR READING! JOIN THE CLUB AND KEEP ON COOKING WITH 6 MORE COOKBOOKS.... 130

Come On.. 132

Let's Be Friends :) 132

ANY ISSUES? CONTACT US

If you find that something important to you is missing from this book please contact us at info@booksumo.com.

We will take your concerns into consideration when the 2nd edition of this book is published. And we will keep you updated!

— BookSumo Press

Legal Notes

ALL RIGHTS RESERVED. NO PART OF THIS BOOK MAY BE REPRODUCED OR TRANSMITTED IN ANY FORM OR BY ANY MEANS. PHOTOCOPYING, POSTING ONLINE, AND / OR DIGITAL COPYING IS STRICTLY PROHIBITED UNLESS WRITTEN PERMISSION IS GRANTED BY THE BOOK'S PUBLISHING COMPANY. LIMITED USE OF THE BOOK'S TEXT IS PERMITTED FOR USE IN REVIEWS WRITTEN FOR THE PUBLIC.

COMMON ABBREVIATIONS

cup(s)	C.
tablespoon	tbsp
teaspoon	tsp
ounce	oz.
pound	lb

*All units used are standard American measurements

Chapter 1: Easy Caramel Recipes

Opera Playhouse Popcorn

Ingredients

- 1 C. butter
- 2 C. brown sugar
- 1/2 C. corn syrup
- 1 tsp salt
- 1/2 tsp baking soda
- 1 tsp vanilla extract
- 5 quarts popped popcorn

Directions

- Set your oven to 250 degrees F before doing anything else.
- In a very large bowl, place the popcorn.
- In a medium pan, melt the butter on medium heat.
- Stir in the brown sugar, corn syrup and salt and bring to a boil, stirring continuously.
- Boil for about 4 minutes without stirring.
- Remove from the heat and immediately, stir in the soda and vanilla.

- Slowly, pour the caramel over the popcorn in a thin stream, stirring continuously.
- Divide the mixture in 2 large shallow baking dishes evenly.
- Cook in the oven for about 1 hour, stirring after every 15 minutes.
- Remove from the oven and keep aside to cool completely before breaking into pieces.

Amount per serving (20 total)

Timing Information:

Preparation	30 m
Cooking	1 h
Total Time	1 h 30 m

Nutritional Information:

Calories	253 kcal
Fat	14 g
Carbohydrates	32.8g
Protein	0.9 g
Cholesterol	24 mg
Sodium	340 mg

* Percent Daily Values are based on a 2,000 calorie diet.

Crusty Caramel Crisps

Ingredients

- 1 C. butter or margarine
- 1 lb. light brown sugar
- 1 (14 oz.) can sweetened condensed milk
- 1 C. light corn syrup
- 1 pinch salt
- 1 1/2 tsp vanilla extract

Directions

- In a heavy-bottomed pan, mix together the butter, brown sugar, sweetened condensed milk, corn syrup and salt on medium heat and bring to a boil, stirring continuously.
- Cook till the temperature reaches between 234-240 degrees F.
- Cook for about 2 minutes.
- Remove from the heat and immediately, stir in vanilla.
- Meanwhile, grease a 13x9-inch baking dish with some melted butter.
- Transfer the caramel into the prepared baking dish evenly and keep aside in the room temperature to cool completely.

- Remove from the baking dish and cut into desired sized squares.
- Wrap these squares in waxed paper and preserve in refrigerator by placing in an airtight container.

Amount per serving (32 total)

Timing Information:

Preparation	10 m
Cooking	30 m
Total Time	40 m

Nutritional Information:

Calories	174 kcal
Fat	6.8 g
Carbohydrates	28.5g
Protein	1 g
Cholesterol	19 mg
Sodium	67 mg

* Percent Daily Values are based on a 2,000 calorie diet.

Autumn Pastry

Ingredients

- 1 pastry for a 9-inch double-crust pie, divided
- 10 apples - peeled, cored, and sliced
- 1 1/2 C. white sugar
- 2 tbsp all-purpose flour
- 1 tbsp ground cinnamon
- 10 individually wrapped caramels, unwrapped
- 3 tbsp butter, sliced
- Topping:
- 1 tbsp milk
- 1 tbsp confectioners' sugar

Directions

- Set your oven to 350 degrees F before doing anything else.
- In the bottom of a 13x9-inch baking dish, arrange a pastry for 1 1/2 pie shells, cutting the pastry to fit and filling gaps as necessary.
- Cut the remaining pie pastry into 1-2-inch pieces.
- In a large bowl, add the apples, sugar, flour and cinnamon and toss to coat well.
- Place the apple mixture over the pie crust and top with the caramels and butter slices.

- Arrange the remaining pie pastry pieces over the caramels and butter.
- Cook in the oven for about 1 hour.
- Remove from the oven and keep onto a wire rack to cool for about 30 minutes.
- Now, remove from baking dish and cut into equal sized bars.
- In a small bowl, add the milk and confectioner's sugar and beat well.
- Drizzle the milk mixture over the bars and serve.

Amount per serving (12 total)

Timing Information:

Preparation	30 m
Cooking	1 h
Total Time	1 h 55 m

Nutritional Information:

Calories	375 kcal
Fat	13.8 g
Carbohydrates	63.2g
Protein	2.8 g
Cholesterol	8 mg
Sodium	199 mg

* Percent Daily Values are based on a 2,000 calorie diet.

Lunch Box Oat Squares

Ingredients

- 32 individually wrapped caramels, unwrapped
- 5 tbsp heavy cream
- 1 C. all-purpose flour
- 1 C. rolled oats
- 3/4 C. brown sugar
- 1/2 tsp baking soda
- 1/4 tsp salt
- 3/4 C. butter, melted
- 1/2 C. semisweet chocolate chips
- 1/2 C. chopped walnuts

Directions

- Set your oven to 350 degrees F before doing anything else.
- In a medium pan, add the caramels and heavy cream on low heat and cook till melted completely, stirring occasionally.
- In a medium bowl, mix together the flour, oats, brown sugar, baking soda and salt.
- Add the melted butter and mix till well combined.
- For crust, place 1/2 of the mixture in the bottom of a 13x9-inch baking dish evenly.

- Cook in the oven for about 8 minutes.
- Remove the baking dish from the oven.
- Sprinkle the chocolate chips and walnuts over the crust, followed by the caramel mixture and the remaining crumble evenly.
- Cook in the oven for about 12 minutes.
- Remove from the oven and keep aside to cool slightly.
- Cut into desired sized squares and serve.

Amount per serving (24 total)

Timing Information:

Preparation	20 m
Cooking	12 m
Total Time	35 m

Nutritional Information:

Calories	195 kcal
Fat	10.9 g
Carbohydrates	23.7g
Protein	2.2 g
Cholesterol	20 mg
Sodium	127 mg

* Percent Daily Values are based on a 2,000 calorie diet.

Caramel Bars

Ingredients

- 16 graham crackers
- 2 C. miniature marshmallows, optional
- 3/4 C. butter
- 1 tsp vanilla extract
- 3/4 C. brown sugar
- 2 C. sliced almonds
- 2 C. flaked coconut

Directions

- Set your oven to 450 degrees F before doing anything else and line a 10x15 inch jellyroll pan with a piece of the foil.
- For crust in the bottom of the prepared pan, place the graham crackers evenly.
- In a small pan, add the butter and brown sugar on medium heat and cook till smooth, stirring occasionally.
- Remove from the heat and immediately, stir in the vanilla.
- Place the marshmallows over the graham cracker crust and top with the butter mixture, followed by the coconut and almonds evenly.
- Cook in the oven for about 14 minutes.

- Remove from the oven and keep aside to cool completely before cutting into triangles.
- Wrap these triangles in waxed paper and preserve at room temperature by placing in an airtight container.

Amount per serving (48 total)

Timing Information:

Preparation	15 m
Cooking	15 m
Total Time	30 m

Nutritional Information:

Calories	114 kcal
Fat	7.9 g
Carbohydrates	10.4g
Protein	1.5 g
Cholesterol	8 mg
Sodium	53 mg

* Percent Daily Values are based on a 2,000 calorie diet.

Aunty Pari's Brownies

Ingredients

- 1 (18.25 oz.) package German chocolate cake mix with pudding
- 3/4 C. melted butter
- 1/3 C. evaporated milk
- 1 C. chopped pecans
- 13 oz. individually wrapped caramels, unwrapped
- 1/3 C. evaporated milk
- 1 C. semi-sweet chocolate chips

Directions

- Set your oven to 350 degrees F before doing anything else and grease a 13x9-inch baking dish.
- In a bowl, add the cake mix, butter and 1/3 C. of the evaporated milk and mix well.
- Place about 2/3 of the cake mix mixture into the prepared baking dish evenly and top with the pecans by pressing slightly.
- Cook in the oven for about 8-10 minutes.
- Remove from the oven and keep aside to cool completely.

- In a pan, mix together the caramel and 1/3 C. of the evaporated milk on medium heat and cook till melted completely, stirring continuously.
- Place the melted caramel mixture over the cooled crust and top with the chocolate chips and remaining cake mix mixture.
- Cook in the oven for about 15-18 minutes.
- Remove from the oven and keep aside to cool completely.
- Then cut into desired sized squares and serve.

Amount per serving (24 total)

Timing Information:

Preparation	20 m
Cooking	1 h 10 m
Total Time	1 h 30 m

Nutritional Information:

Calories	269 kcal
Fat	14 g
Carbohydrates	34.9g
Protein	3.1 g
Cholesterol	18 mg
Sodium	244 mg

* Percent Daily Values are based on a 2,000 calorie diet.

Caramel Coffee Candies

Ingredients

- 1 tsp butter
- 1 C. butter
- 1 (16 oz.) package brown sugar
- 1 (14 oz.) can sweetened condensed milk
- 1 C. light corn syrup
- 3 tbsp instant coffee granules
- 1 C. chopped walnuts
- 1 tsp vanilla extract
- 1/2 tsp orange zest

Directions

- Line an 8-inch square baking dish with a piece of the foil and then grease with about 1 tsp of the melted butter.
- In a pan, melt 1 C. of the butter on medium-low heat.
- Add the brown sugar, sweetened condensed milk, corn syrup and coffee granules and cook for about 20 minutes, stirring continuously.
- Remove from the heat and stir in the walnuts, vanilla extract and orange zest.

- Place the caramel mixture into the prepared baking dish evenly and keep aside in room temperature to cool completely.
- Remove caramel from the baking dish and remove the foil.
- Cut the caramels into squares and serve.

Amount per serving (48 total)

Timing Information:

Preparation	10 m
Cooking	20 m
Total Time	1 h

Nutritional Information:

Calories	132 kcal
Fat	6.2 g
Carbohydrates	19.3g
Protein	1.1 g
Cholesterol	13 mg
Sodium	45 mg

* Percent Daily Values are based on a 2,000 calorie diet.

Caramel Chops

Ingredients

- 3 C. all-purpose flour
- 1 tsp cream of tartar
- 1/2 tsp baking soda
- 1/4 tsp ground nutmeg
- 1 C. shortening, melted and cooled slightly
- 2 C. packed brown sugar
- 2 eggs
- 1 tsp vanilla extract

Directions

- In a bowl, mix together the flour, cream of tartar, baking soda and nutmeg.
- In another large bowl, add the melted shortening and brown sugar and beat till well combined.
- Add the eggs and vanilla extract and beat till well combined.
- Slowly, add the egg mixture into the four mixture and mix till a dough forms.
- Make about 1 1/2-inch log from the dough and wrap in a waxed paper.
- Refrigerate the wrapped log for about overnight.

- Set your oven to 375 degrees F and lightly grease 2 baking sheets.
- Cut the log into 1/4-inch thick slices.
- Arrange the log slices onto the prepared baking sheets in a single layer about 1-inch apart.
- Cook in the oven for about 8-10 minutes.
- Remove from the oven and keep onto wire racks to cool.

Amount per serving (24 total)

Timing Information:

Preparation	10 m
Cooking	1 h
Total Time	1 h 10 m

Nutritional Information:

Calories	209 kcal
Fat	9.1 g
Carbohydrates	30.1g
Protein	2.2 g
Cholesterol	16 mg
Sodium	38 mg

* Percent Daily Values are based on a 2,000 calorie diet.

3-Ingredient Patty Pie

Ingredients

- 1 (14 oz.) can sweetened condensed milk
- 1 (9 inch) prepared graham cracker crust
- 1 (12 oz.) container frozen whipped topping, thawed

Directions

- Remove the label from the cans of milk and arrange into a large pan with a few inches of water.
- Bring to a boil on high heat.
- Reduce the heat to medium-high and cook for about 4 hours, adding water to keep the can covered.
- Remove the can from the boiling water and keep aside to cool.
- Carefully open the can and transfer the browned milk into the pie shell.
- Refrigerate to cool completely.
- Serve with a topping of the frozen whipped topping.

Amount per serving (10 total)

Timing Information:

Preparation	20 m
Cooking	4 h 20 m
Total Time	4 h 40 m

Nutritional Information:

Calories	336 kcal
Fat	17.1 g
Carbohydrates	42.8g
Protein	4.4 g
Cholesterol	13 mg
Sodium	178 mg

* Percent Daily Values are based on a 2,000 calorie diet.

A 3ʳᴅ Grader's Lunch Box Snack

Ingredients

- 1 C. butter
- 2 C. white sugar
- 1 (14 oz.) can sweetened condensed milk
- 1 C. corn syrup
- 1/8 tsp salt
- 1 tsp anise extract
- black paste food coloring

Directions

- Line a 9x9-inch baking dish with a buttered piece of the foil.
- In a large pan, melt the butter on medium heat.
- Add the sugar, milk, corn syrup and salt and bring to a boil, stirring continuously.
- Boil without stirring till the temperature reaches to 242-248 degrees F. (
- Remove from heat and stir in the anise extract and food coloring.
- Transfer the mixture into the prepared baking dish and keep aside to cool completely.

- Carefully, remove the caramel mixture from the baking dish and discard the foil.
- With a buttered knife, cut into desired squares.
- Wrap these squares in waxed paper and preserve in refrigerator by placing in an airtight container.

Amount per serving (64 total)

Timing Information:

Preparation	10 m
Cooking	30 m
Total Time	3 h

Nutritional Information:

Calories	84 kcal
Fat	3.4 g
Carbohydrates	13.5g
Protein	0.5 g
Cholesterol	10 mg
Sodium	36 mg

* Percent Daily Values are based on a 2,000 calorie diet.

Arabian Dream Grapes

Ingredients

- 2 C. sour cream
- 1/2 C. confectioners' sugar
- 2 tbsp vanilla extract
- 5 C. green seedless grapes
- 1 C. butter
- 1 C. brown sugar

Directions

- In a large bowl, add the sour cream, confectioner's sugar and vanilla and mix well.
- Stir in the grapes and keep aside.
- In a medium pan, add the butter and brown sugar on medium heat and cook till mixture becomes thick, stirring continuously.
- Place the brown sugar mixture over the grape mixture and stir till well combined.
- Refrigerate to chill for at least 2 hours before serving.

Amount per serving (12 total)

Timing Information:

Preparation	5 m
Cooking	10 m
Total Time	2 h 15 m

Nutritional Information:

Calories	337 kcal
Fat	23.8 g
Carbohydrates	30.8g
Protein	1.8 g
Cholesterol	58 mg
Sodium	134 mg

* Percent Daily Values are based on a 2,000 calorie diet.

London Street Cookies

Ingredients

- 1/2 C. butter, room temperature
- 2 C. packed brown sugar
- 3 eggs
- 1/2 tsp vanilla extract
- 3 1/2 C. all-purpose flour
- 1/2 tsp baking soda
- 1 tsp cream of tartar
- 1/2 tsp salt
- 1 C. chopped walnuts

Directions

- In a large bowl, add the butter and brown sugar and beat till smooth.
- Add the eggs, one at a time and beat till well combined.
- Stir in the vanilla.
- In another bowl, sift together the flour, baking soda, cream of tartar and salt.
- Add the flour mixture into the egg mixture and mix till well combined.
- Fold in the walnuts.

- Make about a 2-inch log from the dough and wrap in waxed paper.
- Refrigerate the wrapped log for overnight.
- Set your oven to 350 degrees F and lightly, grease the cookie sheets.
- Unwrap the dough roll and with a sharp knife, cut into 1/4-inch thick slices.
- Arrange the log slices onto the prepared cookie sheets in a single layer about 2-inch apart.
- Cook in the oven for about 10-12 minutes.
- Remove from the oven and keep on wire racks to cool.

Amount per serving (24 total)

Timing Information:

Preparation	15 m
Cooking	12 m
Total Time	8 h 20 m

Nutritional Information:

Calories	211 kcal
Fat	7.8 g
Carbohydrates	32.7g
Protein	3.5 g
Cholesterol	33 mg
Sodium	116 mg

* Percent Daily Values are based on a 2,000 calorie diet.

Easy Caramel Cookbook

4-Ingredient Dessert Glaze

Ingredients

- 1/4 C. butter
- 3/4 C. brown sugar
- 1/4 C. heavy cream
- 2 C. confectioners' sugar

Directions

- In a heavy pan, add the butter and brown sugar on medium-low heat and cook the sugar till it dissolves.
- Stir in the cream and bring to a boil.
- Boil for about 1 minute and remove from the heat.
- Keep aside to cool.
- Add the powdered sugar and beat till smooth.

Amount per serving (12 total)

Timing Information:

Preparation	8 m
Cooking	2 m
Total Time	25 m

Nutritional Information:

Calories	163 kcal
Fat	5.7 g
Carbohydrates	29g
Protein	0.2 g
Cholesterol	< 17 mg
Sodium	32 mg

* Percent Daily Values are based on a 2,000 calorie diet.

3-Ingredient Apples

Ingredients

- 6 apples
- 1 (14 oz.) package individually wrapped caramels, unwrapped
- 2 tbsp milk

Directions

- Remove the stem from each apple and insert a craft stick into the top.
- Grease a baking sheet with some melted butter.
- In a microwave safe bowl, add the caramels and milk and microwave for about 2 minutes, stirring once in the middle way.
- Remove from the microwave and keep aside to cool slightly.
- Coat each apple in caramel sauce completely.
- Arrange onto prepared baking sheet to set completely.

Amount per serving (6 total)

Timing Information:

Preparation	8 m
Cooking	2 m
Total Time	25 m

Nutritional Information:

Calories	324 kcal
Fat	5.6 g
Carbohydrates	69.6g
Protein	3.5 g
Cholesterol	5 mg
Sodium	164 mg

* Percent Daily Values are based on a 2,000 calorie diet.

Scottish Bread

Ingredients

- 1/2 C. butter
- 1/4 C. white sugar
- 1 C. all-purpose flour
- 1/4 C. ground almonds
- 3/4 C. butter
- 3/8 C. white sugar
- 3 tbsp golden syrup
- 1 (14 oz.) can sweetened condensed milk
- 8 (1 oz.) squares high quality milk chocolate
- 1/3 C. toasted and sliced almonds

Directions

- Set your oven to 350 degrees F before doing anything else and line an 8-inch square baking dish with a parchment paper.
- In a bowl add 1/2 C. of the butter and 1/4 C. of the sugar and beat till pale.
- Add the flour and ground almonds and mix till a soft dough forms.
- Place the dough in the prepared dish and press to smooth the surface.

- Cook in the oven for about 20-25 minutes.
- Remove from the oven and keep aside to cool.
- For topping in a pan, add 3/4 C. of the butter, 3/8 C. of the sugar, golden syrup and condensed milk on low heat and bring to a boil, stirring continuously.
- Boil for about 5-7 minutes, stirring continuously.
- Pour the caramel over the cooled shortbread and spread evenly.
- Keep aside for about 40 minutes to set.
- In a small pan, melt the chocolate on low heat.
- Spread the melted chocolate over the caramel and sprinkle with the toasted almonds.

Amount per serving (16 total)

Timing Information:

Preparation	20 m
Cooking	1 h
Total Time	1 h 20 m

Nutritional Information:

Calories	380 kcal
Fat	23.4 g
Carbohydrates	39.3g
Protein	5.1 g
Cholesterol	50 mg
Sodium	147 mg

* Percent Daily Values are based on a 2,000 calorie diet.

Caramel Country Bars

Ingredients

- 1 (14 oz.) package individually wrapped caramels, unwrapped
- 3/4 C. shortening
- 2/3 C. evaporated milk, divided
- 1 (18.25 oz.) package German chocolate cake mix
- 1 C. chopped peanuts
- 1 C. semisweet chocolate chips

Directions

- Set your oven to 350 degrees F before doing anything else and grease a 9-inch square baking dish.
- In a bowl, add the shortening and cake mix and mix till smooth.
- Add 1/3 C. of the milk and peanuts and mix till a crumbly mixture forms.
- Place half of the mixture in the prepared baking dish and press to smooth.
- Cook in the oven for about 8 minutes.
- In the top of a double boiler, add the caramels and remaining 1/3 C. of the evaporated milk on low heat and melt till smooth, stirring continuously.

- Remove from the heat and keep aside to cool slightly.
- Sprinkle the chocolate chips over the warm dough.
- Place the caramel mixture over the chocolate chips and sprinkle with the remaining cake mix mixture.
- Cook in the oven for about 18-20 minutes.
- Remove from the oven and keep aside to cool before cutting into bars.

Amount per serving (24 total)

Timing Information:

Preparation	15 m
Cooking	20 m
Total Time	35 m

Nutritional Information:

Calories	282 kcal
Fat	14.6 g
Carbohydrates	36.3g
Protein	4 g
Cholesterol	3 mg
Sodium	207 mg

* Percent Daily Values are based on a 2,000 calorie diet.

1-Ingredient Caramel Sauce

Ingredients

- 1 (14 oz.) can sweetened condensed milk

Directions

- In a large pan of boiling water, place the can of milk, unopened on medium heat.
- Simmer, covered for about 3 hours, turning the can every half hour and adding water to keep the can covered.
- Carefully open the can and serve.

Amount per serving (14 total)

Timing Information:

Preparation	
Cooking	3 h
Total Time	3 h

Nutritional Information:

Calories	90 kcal
Fat	2.4 g
Carbohydrates	15.2g
Protein	2.2 g
Cholesterol	10 mg
Sodium	36 mg

* Percent Daily Values are based on a 2,000 calorie diet.

Valentine's Day Truffle's

Ingredients

- 1 1/4 C. brown sugar
- 1 2/3 C. white sugar
- 1 C. butter
- 1 C. corn syrup
- 1 1/4 C. heavy cream
- 3/4 C. whole milk
- 2 tsp vanilla extract

Directions

- In a medium pan, mix together the brown sugar, white sugar, butter, corn syrup, cream, milk and vanilla on medium heat.
- Cook till the temperature reaches to 250-265 degrees F, stirring occasionally.
- Transfer the mixture into an 8x8-inch baking dish and keep aside to cool before cutting.

Amount per serving (12 total)

Timing Information:

Preparation	
Cooking	20 m
Total Time	45 m

Nutritional Information:

Calories	504 kcal
Fat	25 g
Carbohydrates	72.7g
Protein	1.2 g
Cholesterol	76 mg
Sodium	148 mg

* Percent Daily Values are based on a 2,000 calorie diet.

Cream Cheese Caramel Candy

Ingredients

- 6 oz. cream cheese
- 2 C. all-purpose flour
- 1 C. butter
- 1 (14 oz.) package individually wrapped caramels
- 1/2 C. evaporated milk
- 1/2 C. white sugar
- 1 C. shortening
- 1/3 C. evaporated milk
- 1 tsp vanilla extract

Directions

- Set your oven to 375 degrees F before doing anything else.
- In an owl, add the cream cheese, butter and flour and mix till a dough forms.
- Divide the dough in 48 equal pieces and press into the mini tassie pans.
- Cook in the oven for about 15 minutes.
- Remove from the oven and keep on wire racks to cool slightly.
- Careful, remove the shells from the pans.

- In a microwave safe bowl, add the caramels and 1/2 C. of the evaporated milk and microwave on medium-high heat till melted.
- Remove from the microwave and stir till creamy.
- For frosting in a bowl, add the sugar, 1/3 C. of the evaporated milk, shortening and vanilla and beat till light and creamy.
- Place the melted caramel into shells evenly and top with the frosting.

Amount per serving (48 total)

Timing Information:

Preparation	30 m
Cooking	15 m
Total Time	45 m

Nutritional Information:

Calories	148 kcal
Fat	10.4 g
Carbohydrates	12.9g
Protein	1.5 g
Cholesterol	16 mg
Sodium	62 mg

* Percent Daily Values are based on a 2,000 calorie diet.

Pre-Colonial Candy

Ingredients

- 6 C. white sugar, divided
- 2 C. heavy cream
- 1/2 tsp baking soda
- 1/2 C. butter
- 1 tsp vanilla extract
- 2 lb. pecan halves

Directions

- Grease a 13x9-inch baking dish with a little melted butter.
- Grease a medium, heavy pan with a little melted butter.
- In the greased pan, mix together 4 C. of the sugar and the cream and keep aside.
- In a large heavy skillet, add the remaining 2 C. of the sugar on medium heat and cook till the sugar begins to melt, stirring continuously.
- Place the pan of cream mixture on low heat and cook, stirring occasionally.
- Cook and stir the sugar in the skillet till it is melted completely and light brown.
- Slowly, place the melted sugar into the lightly simmering cream mixture in a thin stream, stirring continuously.

- Now cook till the temperature reaches to 242-248 degrees F, without stirring. (
- Remove from the heat and stir in the baking soda.
- Add the butter in the mixture and keep aside for about 30 minutes, without stirring.
- Add the vanilla and with a wooden spoon, stir vigorously for about 10-15 minutes.
- Fold in the pecans and immediately, transfer the candy into the prepared baking dish.
- Keep aside to cool slightly.
- Cut the warm candy in 1-inch pieces and serve.

Amount per serving (117 total)

Timing Information:

Preparation	30 m
Cooking	45 m
Total Time	2 h

Nutritional Information:

Calories	114 kcal
Fat	7.9 g
Carbohydrates	11.4g
Protein	0.8 g
Cholesterol	8 mg
Sodium	13 mg

* Percent Daily Values are based on a 2,000 calorie diet.

Winter Carnival Popcorn

Ingredients

- 11 C. popped popcorn
- 1 C. Spanish peanuts
- 1 1/4 C. dark brown sugar
- 10 tbsp unsalted butter, cut into pieces
- 1/4 C. dark corn syrup
- 1 tsp kosher salt

Directions

- Set your oven to 250 degrees F before doing anything else.
- In the bottom of a large, deep roasting pan, place the popcorn and top with the peanuts.
- In a pan, mix together the brown sugar, butter, corn syrup and salt on medium-high heat and cook for about 2-3 minutes, beating continuously.
- Immediately, place the caramel sauce over the popcorn and peanuts and stir to coat completely.
- Cook in the oven for about 45 minutes, stirring occasionally.
- Remove from the oven and transfer the popcorn mixture onto a large parchment paper in a single layer to cool completely.

Amount per serving (11 total)

Timing Information:

Preparation	15 m
Cooking	50 m
Total Time	1 h 35 m

Nutritional Information:

Calories	349 kcal
Fat	21.8 g
Carbohydrates	37.4g
Protein	4.4 g
Cholesterol	28 mg
Sodium	314 mg

* Percent Daily Values are based on a 2,000 calorie diet.

Margarita's Flan

Ingredients

- 3/4 C. white sugar
- 1 (8 oz.) package cream cheese, softened
- 5 eggs
- 1 (14 oz.) can sweetened condensed milk
- 1 (12 fluid oz.) can evaporated milk
- 1 tsp vanilla extract

Directions

- Set your oven to 350 degrees F before doing anything else.
- In a small, heavy pan, add the sugar on medium-low heat and cook till golden, stirring continuously.
- Transfer the mixture into a 10-inch round baking dish and tilt to coat the bottom and sides.
- In a large bowl, add the cream cheese and beat till smooth.
- Add the eggs, one at a time and beat till well combined.
- Add the condensed milk, evaporated milk and vanilla and beat till smooth.
- Place the milk mixture into the caramel coated baking dish.

- Arrange the baking dish in a damp kitchen towel lined roasting pan.
- Arrange the roasting pan on oven rack.
- Add the boiling water in the roasting pan to reach halfway up the sides of the baking dish.
- Cook in the oven for about 50-60 minutes.
- Remove from the oven and keep onto wire rack for about 1 hour.
- Refrigerate for about 8 hours or overnight.
- Carefully, run a knife around the edges of pan and invert on a rimmed serving platter.

Amount per serving (10 total)

Timing Information:

Preparation	15 m
Cooking	1 h 15 m
Total Time	8 h

Nutritional Information:

Calories	350 kcal
Fat	16.6 g
Carbohydrates	41g
Protein	10.5 g
Cholesterol	142 mg
Sodium	191 mg

* Percent Daily Values are based on a 2,000 calorie diet.

Asian Fusion Sweet Chicken

Ingredients

- 3/4 C. dark brown sugar
- 1/3 C. cold water
- 1/3 C. fish sauce
- 1/3 C. rice vinegar
- 1 tbsp soy sauce
- 4 cloves garlic, crushed
- 1 tbsp fresh grated ginger
- 1 tsp vegetable oil
- 8 boneless, skinless chicken thighs, quartered
- 1/2 C. roasted peanuts
- 2 fresh jalapeno peppers, seeded and sliced
- 1 bunch green onions, chopped
- fresh cilantro sprigs, for garnish

Directions

- In a bowl, add the brown sugar, water, fish sauce, rice vinegar, soy sauce, garlic and ginger and beat till the brown sugar is dissolved completely.
- In a skillet, heat the oil on high heat and stir in the chicken.

- Place about 1/3 C. of the brown sugar mixture over the chicken and cook for about 6-7 minutes.
- Place the remaining brown sugar mixture and cook for about 5 minutes.
- Stir in in the peanuts, jalapeños and green onion and cook for about 2-3 minutes.
- Serve with a garnishing of the cilantro.

Amount per serving (4 total)

Timing Information:

Preparation	20 m
Cooking	20 m
Total Time	40 m

Nutritional Information:

Calories	615 kcal
Fat	33.2 g
Carbohydrates	37.9g
Protein	43 g
Cholesterol	129 mg
Sodium	1967 mg

* Percent Daily Values are based on a 2,000 calorie diet.

Manhattan Bridge Cheesecake

Ingredients

- 2 C. graham cracker crumbs
- 1/2 C. butter, melted
- 2 tbsp white sugar
- 3 (8 oz.) packages cream cheese, softened
- 1 C. white sugar
- 3 eggs
- 1 (8 oz.) container sour cream
- 1/4 C. brewed espresso
- 2 tsp vanilla extract
- pressurized whipped cream
- caramel ice cream topping

Directions

- Set your oven to 350 degrees F before doing anything else and lightly, grease a 9-inch springform pan.
- In a bowl, mix together the graham cracker crumbs, melted butter and 2 tbsp of the sugar till well combined.
- Place the mixture in the prepared springform pan, and press in the bottom and 1-inch up the sides.
- Cook in the oven for about 8 minutes.
- Remove from the oven and place onto a wire rack to cool.

- Now, set your oven to 325 degrees F.
- In a large bowl, add the softened cream cheese and with an electric mixer, beat till fluffy.
- Slowly, add 1 C. of the sugar, beating till well combined.
- Add the eggs, one at a time, beating till well combined.
- Stir in the sour cream, espresso and vanilla.
- Place the mixture into the cooled crust.
- Cook in the oven for about 65 minutes.
- Turn the oven off and open the door partially and keep the cheesecake inside for about 15 minutes.
- Remove from the oven and carefully, run a knife around the edges.
- Keep on a wire rack in room temperature to cool.
- With a plastic wrap, cover the springform pan and refrigerate for about 8 hours.
- Cut the cheesecake into desired sized wedges and serve with a topping of the whipped cream and caramel sauce.

Amount per serving (12 total)

Timing Information:

Preparation	35 m
Cooking	1 h 28 m
Total Time	10 h 3 m

Nutritional Information:

Calories	486 kcal
Fat	35 g
Carbohydrates	37.1g
Protein	7.7 g
Cholesterol	141 mg
Sodium	363 mg

* Percent Daily Values are based on a 2,000 calorie diet.

Caramel Cream Dream

Ingredients

- cooking spray
- 1/2 C. (scant) white sugar
- 1 large egg
- 3 large egg yolks
- 1/4 tsp salt
- 1/4 C. white sugar
- 1/2 C. crème fraiche
- 1/2 C. whole milk
- 1 tsp vanilla extract
- 1/2 tsp orange cognac, optional

Directions

- Set your oven to 325 degrees F before doing anything else and lightly, grease 4 (6 1/2-oz.) ramekins with cooking spray.
- Arrange the ramekins in a casserole dish.
- In a small, heavy, dry skillet, place 1/2 C. of the sugar on medium heat and cook till the sugar melts completely, shaking the pan continuously.
- Remove the pan from the heat and immediately, place the caramel syrup in the prepared ramekins evenly.

- In a bowl, add 1 egg, 3 egg yolks, a pinch of the salt and 1/4 C. of the sugar and beat till frothy.
- Add the crème fraiche, milk, vanilla and Grand Marnier and beat till well combined.
- Pace the mixture into the prepared ramekins, about 2/3-3/4 full.
- Add the hot water in the casserole dish to reach halfway up the sides of the ramekins.
- Arrange the casserole over the middle rack of the oven.
- Cook in the oven for about 45-50 minutes.
- Transfer the ramekins onto a wire rack to cool slightly.
- Carefully, run a sharp paring knife around the edge of slightly warm custard.
- Place a small plate over each ramekin and invert.
- Refrigerate to chill before serving.

Amount per serving (4 total)

Timing Information:

Preparation	15 m
Cooking	50 m
Total Time	1 h 35 m

Nutritional Information:

Calories	328 kcal
Fat	16.8 g
Carbohydrates	40.8g
Protein	5.5 g
Cholesterol	244 mg
Sodium	191 mg

* Percent Daily Values are based on a 2,000 calorie diet.

Sunday's Breakfast

Ingredients

- 4 tbsp butter, divided
- 6 eggs
- 1/2 C. milk
- 1/8 tsp salt
- 8 slices bread
- 1 C. brown sugar
- 1/2 C. water

Directions

- In a bowl, add the eggs, milk and salt and beat well.
- Dip the bread slices, one at a time into the egg mixture evenly.
- In a skillet, melt 2 tbsp of the butter on medium-high heat and fry 4 bread slices till golden brown from both sides.
- Repeat with the remaining butter and bread slices.
- Transfer the bread slices onto a plate.
- In the same skillet, add the brown sugar and cook till melted and sticky, stirring continuously.
- Stir in the water.
- Add the French toast and gently, coat with the caramel sauce evenly.

- Serve immediately.

Amount per serving (8 total)

Timing Information:

Preparation	10 m
Cooking	20 m
Total Time	30 m

Nutritional Information:

Calories	248 kcal
Fat	10.6 g
Carbohydrates	31.4g
Protein	7.2 g
Cholesterol	156 mg
Sodium	312 mg

* Percent Daily Values are based on a 2,000 calorie diet.

Caramel Coocoo's

Ingredients

- 1/2 C. butter
- 3/4 C. white corn syrup
- 1 C. packed brown sugar
- 1 C. chopped pecans
- 1 C. almonds
- 1 (12 oz.) package crispy corn and rice cereal

Directions

- Set your oven to 275 degrees F before doing anything else and grease a large roasting pan with non-stick cooking spray.
- In a microwave safe bowl, mix together the butter, white corn syrup and brown sugar and microwave for about 2 minutes.
- In the prepared roasting pan, place the cereal, pecans and almonds and top with the melted butter mixture and gently, stir to coat
- Cook in the oven for about 1 hour, stirring after every 15 minutes.
- Remove from the oven and keep aside to cool completely, stirring occasionally.

Amount per serving (20 total)

Timing Information:

Preparation	10 m
Cooking	1 h
Total Time	1 h 10 m

Nutritional Information:

Calories	262 kcal
Fat	12.6 g
Carbohydrates	36.9g
Protein	3.4 g
Cholesterol	12 mg
Sodium	183 mg

* Percent Daily Values are based on a 2,000 calorie diet.

Macho Macchiato

Ingredients

- 1 C. milk
- 2 tbsp instant coffee granules
- 1 C. white sugar
- 1 pinch salt
- 2 C. heavy cream
- 3/4 C. caramel dessert sauce

Directions

- In a large bowl, add the milk, instant coffee granules, sugar and salt and beat till the sugar dissolves.
- Stir in the heavy cream and refrigerate, covered for at least 2 hours.
- Transfer the chilled mixture into an ice cream maker and freeze according to manufacturer's instructions.
- Transfer half of the ice cream to a 1-2 quart plastic container and top with half of the caramel sauce.
- Repeat the layers with the remaining ice cream and caramel sauce.
- With a knife, swirl the caramel into the ice cream.
- With a plastic wrap, cover the container and seal.
- For best results, freeze for at least 2 hours or overnight.

Amount per serving (12 total)

Timing Information:

Preparation	
Cooking	10 m
Total Time	4 h 10 m

Nutritional Information:

Calories	264 kcal
Fat	15.1 g
Carbohydrates	32.3g
Protein	1.8 g
Cholesterol	56 mg
Sodium	127 mg

* Percent Daily Values are based on a 2,000 calorie diet.

Picnic Fudge

Ingredients

BOTTOM LAYER

- 1 C. milk chocolate chips
- 1/4 C. butterscotch chips
- 1/4 C. creamy peanut butter

FILLING

- 1/4 C. butter
- 1 C. white sugar
- 1/4 C. evaporated milk
- 1 1/2 C. marshmallow crème
- 1/4 C. creamy peanut butter
- 1 tsp vanilla extract
- 1 1/2 C. chopped salted peanuts

CARAMEL

- 1 (14 oz.) package individually wrapped caramels, unwrapped
- 1/4 C. heavy cream

TOP LAYER

- 1 C. milk chocolate chips
- 1/4 C. butterscotch chips

- 1/4 C. creamy peanut butter

Directions

- Lightly grease a 13x9-inch baking dish.
- For the bottom layer in a small pan, mix together 1 C. of the milk chocolate chips, 1/4 C. of the butterscotch chips and 1/4 C. of the creamy peanut butter on low heat and cook and till melted and smooth, stirring continuously.
- Transfer the mixture in the prepared baking dish evenly.
- Refrigerate till set.
- For the filling in a heavy pan, melt the butter on medium-high heat.
- Add the sugar and evaporated milk and bring to a boil.
- Boil for about 5 minutes.
- Remove from the heat and stir in marshmallow crème, 1/4 C. of the peanut butter and vanilla.
- Fold in the peanuts.
- Place the filling over the bottom layer evenly and refrigerate till set.
- For the caramel in a medium pan, mix together the caramels and cream on low heat and cook till melted and smooth, stirring continuously.
- Place the caramel mixture over the filling evenly and refrigerate till set.
- For the top layer in a small pan, mix together 1 C. of the milk chocolate chips, 1/4 C. butterscotch chips, and 1/4 C.

peanut butter on low heat and cook and cook till melted and smooth, stirring continuously.
- Place the chocolate mixture over the caramel mixture evenly and refrigerate for about 1 hour.
- Cut into 1-inch squares and serve.

Amount per serving (96 total)

Timing Information:

Preparation	30 m
Cooking	30 m
Total Time	2 h 20 m

Nutritional Information:

Calories	85 kcal
Fat	4.6 g
Carbohydrates	10.1g
Protein	1.5 g
Cholesterol	4 mg
Sodium	50 mg

* Percent Daily Values are based on a 2,000 calorie diet.

How to Make a Caramel Roll

Ingredients

- 2 C. milk
- 2 (.25 oz.) packages active dry yeast
- 1/2 C. warm water
- 1/3 C. white sugar
- 1/3 C. vegetable oil
- 1 tbsp baking powder
- 2 tsp salt
- 1 egg
- 7 C. all-purpose flour
- 1 C. packed brown sugar
- 1/2 C. butter
- 2 tbsp light corn syrup
- 1 C. pecan halves
- 1/4 C. butter, softened
- 1/2 C. white sugar
- 1 1/2 tbsp ground cinnamon

Directions

- In a small pan, warm the milk till just bubbles appear.

- Remove from the heat and keep aside to cool till lukewarm.
- In a small bowl, dissolve the yeast in warm water and keep aside for about 10 minutes.
- In a large bowl, add the yeast mixture, milk, sugar, oil, baking powder, salt, egg and 3 C. of the flour and beat till smooth.
- Slowly, add the remaining flour, 1/2 C. at a time, beating till a sticky dough forms.
- Place the dough onto a lightly floured surface and knead for about 8 minutes.
- Place the dough in a lightly, greased large bowl.
- With a damp cloth, cover the bowl and keep in a warm place for about 1 hour.
- In a pan, add the brown sugar and 1/2 C. of the butter and cook till melted, stirring continuously.
- Remove from the heat and stir in the corn syrup.
- Divide the mixture between 2 (13x9-inch) inch baking dishes evenly and sprinkle with the pecans.
- Now, punch down the dough and place onto a lightly floured surface.
- Roll the dough into a large rectangle.
- Spread the butter over the rectangle and sprinkle with the sugar and cinnamon.
- Starting with the long side, roll up the rectangle into a log.
- Cut the log in 1-inch wide slices and arrange the rolls into the baking dishes in a single layer, slightly apart.

- With a piece of foil, cover the baking dishes and refrigerate for at least 12 hours.
- Remove the rolls from refrigerator and place in a warm place for about 30 minutes.
- Set your oven to 350 degrees F.
- Cook in the oven for about 30-35 minutes.
- Remove from the oven and immediately invert the pans onto the heatproof serving plates.
- After about 2 minutes, remove the rolls from the pans and serve.

Amount per serving (24 total)

Timing Information:

Preparation	1 h 30 m
Cooking	35 m
Total Time	16 h 40 m

Nutritional Information:

Calories	327 kcal
Fat	13.3 g
Carbohydrates	47.4g
Protein	5.5 g
Cholesterol	25 mg
Sodium	293 mg

* Percent Daily Values are based on a 2,000 calorie diet.

Central American Inspired Flan

Ingredients

- 3/4 C. white sugar
- 2 egg yolks
- 6 egg whites
- 1 3/4 C. water
- 1 (14 oz.) can low-fat sweetened condensed milk
- 1/2 tsp vanilla extract
- 1 pinch salt

Directions

- Set your oven to 350 degrees F before doing anything else.
- In a heavy skillet, cook the sugar on medium-low heat till melted and light brown, stirring continuously.
- Carefully, transfer the mixture into a 9-inch round baking dish evenly.
- In a bowl, add the egg yolks and egg whites and beat well.
- Add the water, condensed milk, vanilla and salt and mix till smooth.
- Place into the baking dish over the sugar.
- Arrange the baking dish in a damp kitchen towel lined roasting pan.
- Arrange the roasting pan on oven rack.

- Add the boiling water in the roasting pan to reach halfway up the sides of the baking dish.
- Cook in the oven for about 1 hour.
- Remove the baking dish from the oven and lace onto a wire rack to cool for about 1 hour.
- Refrigerate for about overnight.
- Carefully, run a knife around the edge of the pan and then invert onto a rimmed serving platter.

Amount per serving (8 total)

Timing Information:

Preparation	15 m
Cooking	1 h
Total Time	1 h 15 m

Nutritional Information:

Calories	327 kcal
Fat	3.7 g
Carbohydrates	59.5g
Protein	8.7 g
Cholesterol	60 mg
Sodium	162 mg

* Percent Daily Values are based on a 2,000 calorie diet.

A Simple Cake Topping

Ingredients

- 1 C. brown sugar
- 2 tbsp all-purpose flour
- 3 tbsp butter
- 1/4 C. milk
- 1 tsp vanilla extract
- 1/3 C. toasted, chopped pecans

Directions

- In a shallow 6-inch pan, mix together the brown sugar and flour on medium-high heat.
- Add the butter and milk and bring to a rolling boil.
- Boil for about 1 1/2 minutes.
- Remove from the heat and keep aside to cool for about 5 minutes.
- With a wooden spoon, beat the mixture till it becomes thick.
- Add the vanilla and beat for about 1-2 minutes.
- Immediately, place the caramel frosting over the cooled cake and with the back of a warm spoon, spread evenly.
- Sprinkle the toasted pecan on top and keep aside for till the frosting is set.

Amount per serving (24 total)

Timing Information:

Preparation	30 m
Cooking	5 m
Total Time	40 m

Nutritional Information:

Calories	62 kcal
Fat	2.6 g
Carbohydrates	9.8g
Protein	0.3 g
Cholesterol	< 4 mg
Sodium	14 mg

* Percent Daily Values are based on a 2,000 calorie diet.

Canadian Country Apple Crisp

Ingredients

- 1/2 C. caramel topping
- 1/2 tsp ground cinnamon
- 6 large baking apples, peeled and cut into 1/2-inch slices
- 2/3 C. all-purpose flour
- 1/2 C. packed brown sugar
- 1/2 C. cold butter, cut into small pieces
- 2/3 C. quick cooking oats

Directions

- Set your oven to 375 degrees F before doing anything else.
- In a bowl, mix together the caramel topping and cinnamon.
- Add the apples and toss to coat well.
- In another bowl, mix together the flour and brown sugar.
- With a pastry cutter, cut in the butter till a coarse crumbs like mixture forms.
- Stir in the oats.
- In the bottom of an 8-inch square baking dish, place the apple mixture evenly and top with oat mixture.
- Cook in the oven for about 45-50 minutes.

Amount per serving (6 total)

Timing Information:

Preparation	20 m
Cooking	45 m
Total Time	1 h 5 m

Nutritional Information:

Calories	469 kcal
Fat	16.5 g
Carbohydrates	82g
Protein	3.8 g
Cholesterol	41 mg
Sodium	212 mg

* Percent Daily Values are based on a 2,000 calorie diet.

STATE FAIR APPLES

Ingredients

- 2 large Granny Smith apples, peeled
- 4-inch lollipop sticks
- 1 (11 oz.) package individually wrapped caramels, unwrapped
- 2 tbsp milk
- 3 tbsp chopped nuts

Directions

- Line a baking sheet with a waxed paper.
- With a melon baller, scoop 6-8 balls from each apple.
- With paper towels, pat dry the apple balls.
- Place the apple balls onto the prepared baking sheet.
- Insert a lollipop stick in each apple ball and refrigerate till the caramel is prepared.
- In a pan, add the caramels and milk on medium-low heat and cook for about 3-4 minutes, stirring continuously.
- Remove from the heat and keep aside to cool for about 5 minutes.
- In a shallow dish, place the nuts.
- Dip the apple pops in the cooled caramel and let the excess caramel to drip back into pan.

- Now, coat the pops in the nuts evenly and arrange onto the waxed paper lined baking sheet, stick-side up.

Amount per serving (16 total)

Timing Information:

Preparation	15 m
Cooking	5 m
Total Time	25 m

Nutritional Information:

Calories	96 kcal
Fat	2.5 g
Carbohydrates	18.6g
Protein	1.3 g
Cholesterol	2 mg
Sodium	< 49 mg

* Percent Daily Values are based on a 2,000 calorie diet.

Catalina's Crazy Custard

Ingredients

- 9 large egg yolks
- 2/3 C. white sugar
- 2 C. heavy cream
- 1/2 tsp kosher salt
- 2 tsp vanilla extract
- 1 C. whole milk
- Flaky sea salt, to garnish

Directions

- Set your oven to 300 degrees F before doing anything else.
- Arrange 6 (6 1/2-oz.) ramekins in a baking dish.
- In the bottom of a heavy-bottomed pan, place the sugar evenly on medium heat.
- Let the sugar melt for about 5 minutes, without stirring and adjusting the heat if necessary.
- When edges start to bubble, shake and swirl the pan to dissolve the remaining sugar, without stirring.
- Cook for about 10 minutes, shaking the pan occasionally.
- Add the cream and beat well.

- Cook on medium heat ti the caramel melts and sugar dissolves completely, stirring continuously.
- Remove from heat and stir in the kosher salt, vanilla and cold milk till well combined.
- In a large bowl, add the egg yolks and add the caramel mixture, a ladleful at a time, beating till well combined.
- Place the custard mixture into the ramekins evenly.
- Carefully, place the enough water in the baking dish so that it comes halfway up the sides of the ramekins.
- Cook in the oven for about 45-60 minutes.
- Remove from the oven and place the ramekins onto a wire rack to cool.
- With the plastic wraps, cover the ramekins and refrigerate for at least 1 hour to chill.
- Sprinkle with a pinch of light, flaky sea salt and serve.

Amount per serving (6 total)

Timing Information:

Preparation	10 m
Cooking	1 h
Total Time	2 h 10 m

Nutritional Information:

Calories	467 kcal
Fat	37.3 g
Carbohydrates	27.3g
Protein	6.9 g
Cholesterol	420 mg
Sodium	272 mg

* Percent Daily Values are based on a 2,000 calorie diet.

Deluxe French Toast 101

Ingredients

- 1 C. brown sugar
- 1/2 C. butter
- 2 tbsp light corn syrup
- 1/4 C. pecan halves (optional)
- 1 apple, sliced (optional)
- 12 slices bread
- 6 eggs, beaten
- 1 1/2 C. milk
- 1 tsp vanilla extract
- 1/2 tsp almond extract
- 1/4 tsp salt

Directions

- Grease a 13x9-inch baking dish.
- In a pan, add the brown sugar, butter and corn syrup on medium heat and cook for about 5 minutes, stirring occasionally.
- Meanwhile in a bowl, add the eggs, milk, vanilla extract, almond extract and salt and beat till well combined.

- Place the butter mixture into the prepared baking dish and top with the pecans, followed by the apple slices and bread slices.
- Spread the egg mixture over the bread slices evenly and keep in room temperature for about 1 hour.
- Set your oven to 350 degrees F.
- Cook in the oven for about 40-45 minutes.

Amount per serving (10 total)

Timing Information:

Preparation	15 m
Cooking	45 m
Total Time	2 h

Nutritional Information:

Calories	344 kcal
Fat	15.9 g
Carbohydrates	43.8g
Protein	7.7 g
Cholesterol	139 mg
Sodium	394 mg

* Percent Daily Values are based on a 2,000 calorie diet.

Lover's Movie-Time Popcorn

Ingredients

- 23 large marshmallows, optional
- 2 C. brown sugar
- 1/4 C. light corn syrup
- 1 C. butter
- 1 tsp vanilla extract
- 2 (3.5 oz.) packages microwave popcorn, popped

Directions

- In a pan, add the marshmallows, brown sugar, corn syrup, butter and vanilla extract on medium-low heat and cook for about 5 to 7 minutes, stirring occasionally.
- In a large bowl, place the popcorn.
- Place the marshmallow mixture over the popcorn and gently stir to combine.

Amount per serving (8 total)

Timing Information:

Preparation	5 m
Cooking	15 m
Total Time	20 m

Nutritional Information:

Calories	562 kcal
Fat	30 g
Carbohydrates	74.5g
Protein	2.9 g
Cholesterol	61 mg
Sodium	416 mg

* Percent Daily Values are based on a 2,000 calorie diet.

NUTTY CAKE FROM MUNICH

Ingredients

- 1 (18.25 oz.) package German chocolate cake mix
- 1 C. semisweet chocolate chips
- 1 (5 oz.) can evaporated milk
- 14 oz. individually wrapped caramels
- 3/4 C. butter
- 1 C. walnuts

Directions

- Set your oven to 350 degrees F before doing anything else and lightly, grease a 13x9-inch cake pan.
- Prepare the cake mix according to package's instructions.
- Place 1/2 of the cake mixture into the prepared pan evenly.
- Cook in the oven for about 20 minutes.
- In a pan, melt the caramels, margarine, and milk on medium-low heat.
- Place the caramel mixture over the baked cake and top with the chocolate chips, followed by 1/2 of the walnuts, remaining cake mixture and remaining walnuts.
- Cook in the oven for about 20-25 minutes more.

Amount per serving (24 total)

Timing Information:

Preparation	20 m
Cooking	1 h
Total Time	1 h 40 m

Nutritional Information:

Calories	266 kcal
Fat	13.6 g
Carbohydrates	35.5g
Protein	3.1 g
Cholesterol	18 mg
Sodium	246 mg

* Percent Daily Values are based on a 2,000 calorie diet.

SIMPLE LIFE GRAPES

Ingredients

- 2 C. yogurt
- 1/2 C. confectioners' sugar
- 2 tbsp vanilla extract
- 5 C. red seedless grapes
- 1 C. butter
- 1 C. brown sugar

Directions

- In a large bowl, add the yogurt, confectioner's sugar and vanilla and mix well.
- Stir in the grapes and keep aside.
- In a medium pan, add the butter and brown sugar on medium heat and cook till mixture becomes thick, stirring continuously.
- Place the brown sugar mixture over the grape mixture and stir till well combined.
- Refrigerate to chill for at least 2 hours before serving.

Amount per serving (12 total)

Timing Information:

Preparation	5 m
Cooking	10 m
Total Time	2 h 15 m

Nutritional Information:

Calories	337 kcal
Fat	23.8 g
Carbohydrates	30.8g
Protein	1.8 g
Cholesterol	58 mg
Sodium	134 mg

* Percent Daily Values are based on a 2,000 calorie diet.

Cream Cheese Parfait

Ingredients

- 4 oz. Cream Cheese, softened
- 1 1/2 C. cold milk
- 1 (3.4 oz.) package Butterscotch Instant Pudding
- 1 (8 oz.) Whipped Topping, thawed, divided
- 1/2 C. Coffee
- 1/4 C. caramel ice cream topping
- 1 (16 oz.) frozen lb cake, cut into 3/4-inch cubes
- 1 1/2 oz. Semi-Sweet Chocolate, grated

Directions

- Begin to whisk your cream cheese in a bowl for 1 min then slowly add in the milk.
- Stir the milk into the cream then add the pudding mix and continue to work the mix for 60 more secs.
- Now add in 2 C. of whipped topping.
- Get a 2nd bowl, combine: caramel and coffee.
- Grab ten glasses for serving and place half of the cake pieces into them.
- Divide half of the coffee mix and half of the cream cheese mix as well.

- Now divide 1/3 of the grated chocolate between the glasses.
- Continue layering in this manner one more time.
- Add a final layer of whipped topping and chocolate.
- Place everything in the fridge for 5 hrs, with a covering of plastic, then serve.
- Enjoy.

Amount per serving (10 total)

Timing Information:

Preparation	
Cooking	20 m
Total Time	4 h 2 m

Nutritional Information:

Calories	342 kcal
Fat	16.6 g
Carbohydrates	43.6g
Protein	4.5 g
Cholesterol	116 mg
Sodium	423 mg

* Percent Daily Values are based on a 2,000 calorie diet.

Caramel Parfait

Ingredients

- 1/3 C. sugar
- 3 egg yolks
- 4 tbsps dry tapioca
- 3 1/2 C. milk
- 3/4 C. caramel sauce
- 1/4 C. nuts

Directions

- Get a bowl and fill it with ice water.
- Now add the following to a pan: egg yolks, sugar, milk, and tapioca.
- With a medium level of heat, stir and combine the mix until it is boiling.
- Now shut the heat and add the pudding to a bowl.
- Place the bowl in the ice water and let everything sit for 60 mins.
- Add 3 tbsps of tapioca to a parfait glass then add 1 tbsp of preserves.
- Now add 2 more tbsps of tapioca.

- Layer the mix in this manner with 5 more glasses then top each one with cinnamon and chocolate.
- Enjoy.

Amount per serving: 6

Timing Information:

Preparation	30 mins
Total Time	50 mins

Nutritional Information:

Calories	347.3
Cholesterol	115.0mg
Sodium	243.1mg
Carbohydrates	48.7g
Protein	8.6g

* Percent Daily Values are based on a 2,000 calorie diet.

Vanilla Caramel Bars

Ingredients

- 1 1/2 C. Graham Cracker Crumbs
- 1 C. finely chopped pecans, divided
- 1/4 C. butter, melted
- 4 (250 g) packages Cream Cheese, softened
- 1 C. sugar
- 1 C. sour cream
- 1 tbsp vanilla
- 4 eggs
- 1/4 C. caramel ice cream topping

Directions

- Set your oven at 350 degrees before doing anything else.
- Put foil in the pan before pressing a mixture of cracker crumbs, sugar and melted butter into the baking dish.
- Add eggs (one at a time) into a mixture of cream cheese and sugar before adding vanilla and sour cream.
- Mix everything thoroughly.
- Pour this over the crust in the baking dish.
- Bake this in the preheated oven for about 45 minutes.
- Refrigerate it for at least 4 hours.

- Top with caramel and remaining nuts.
- Serve.

Serving: 32

Timing Information:

Preparation	Cooking	Total Time
15 mins	45 mins	5 hr 30 mins

Nutritional Information:

Calories	202 kcal
Carbohydrates	13.8 g
Cholesterol	66 mg
Fat	15.7 g
Fiber	0.4 g
Protein	3.7 g
Sodium	182 mg

* Percent Daily Values are based on a 2,000 calorie diet.

WALNUTS AND CARAMEL

Ingredients

- 1/2 C. butter, room temperature
- 2 C. packed brown sugar
- 3 eggs
- 1/2 tsp vanilla extract
- 3 1/2 C. all-purpose flour
- 1/2 tsp baking soda
- 1 tsp cream of tartar
- 1/2 tsp salt
- 1 C. chopped walnuts

Directions

- Set your oven at 350 degrees F before doing anything else.
- Add a mixture of flour, baking soda, cream of tartar and salt into a mixture of butter, brown sugar, egg and vanilla before forming small sized coins out of it.
- Place these coins with some distance on a baking sheet.
- Bake everything in the preheated oven for about 12 minutes.
- Cool it down.
- Serve.

Serving: 4 dozen

Timing Information:

Preparation	Cooking	Total Time
15 mins	12 mins	8 hr 20 mins

Nutritional Information:

Calories	211 kcal
Carbohydrates	32.7 g
Cholesterol	33 mg
Fat	7.8 g
Fiber	0.8 g
Protein	3.5 g
Sodium	116 mg

* Percent Daily Values are based on a 2,000 calorie diet.

Warm Spiced Popcorn

Ingredients

- 1 C. butter
- 2 C. brown sugar
- 1/2 C. corn syrup
- 1 1/2 tsp salt
- 1 C. shredded coconut, divided
- 1/4 C. chopped peanuts
- 1/4 C. sliced almonds, divided
- 2 tsp vanilla extract
- 1 tsp baking soda
- 1/4 tsp ground cinnamon
- 1 pinch ground nutmeg
- 1 pinch ground allspice
- 2 tbsp virgin coconut oil
- 1 tbsp butter
- 1 tbsp vegetable oil
- 1/2 C. unpopped popcorn
- 3/4 C. chocolate chips
- 1 tbsp virgin coconut oil
- 1 tbsp shortening
- 1 tbsp confectioners' sugar, sifted

Directions

- Set your oven to 250 degrees F before doing anything else and line 2 baking sheets with parchment paper.
- In a pan, melt 1 cup of the butter on medium heat and add the corn syrup, brown sugar and salt.
- Bring to a boil, stirring continuously and reduce the heat to low.
- Simmer for about 4 minutes.
- Remove everything from the heat and immediately, stir in the peanuts, 2 tbsp of the almonds, 1/3 C. of the coconut, vanilla extract, baking soda and spices.
- In a large pan, heat 2 tbsp of the coconut oil, vegetable oil and the remaining butter on high heat and stir in the popcorn.
- Cover the pan and shake continuously till the popping completes.
- Place the caramel sauce over the popcorn mixture and stir to combine.
- Transfer the mixture into prepared baking sheets and top with the remaining almonds and 1/3 C. of the coconut.
- Cook everything in the oven for about 45 minutes.
- Now, set the broiler of your oven to heat and arrange the oven rack about 6-inches from the heat element.
- Now, cook the popcorn mixture under the broiler for about 30 seconds.
- In a small pan, cook the remaining coconut oil, shortening and chocolate chips till melted completely and smooth.

- Pour the melted chocolate mixture over the popcorn mixture evenly.
- Sprinkle with the remaining coconut and confectioner's sugar.
- Remove the parchment from the baking sheets and refrigerate for about 45 minutes.
- Break the dish into the desired size pieces and serve.

Amount per serving (8 total)

Timing Information:

Preparation	15 m
Cooking	50 m
Total Time	1 h 50 m

Nutritional Information:

Calories	789 kcal
Fat	46.2 g
Carbohydrates	97.2g
Protein	4.5 g
Cholesterol	65 mg
Sodium	864 mg

* Percent Daily Values are based on a 2,000 calorie diet.

THANKS FOR READING! JOIN THE CLUB AND KEEP ON COOKING WITH 6 MORE COOKBOOKS....

http://bit.ly/1TdrStv

To grab the box sets simply follow the link mentioned above, or tap one of book covers.

This will take you to a page where you can simply enter your email address and a PDF version of the box sets will be emailed to you.

Hope you are ready for some serious cooking!

http://bit.ly/1TdrStv

COME ON...
LET'S BE FRIENDS :)

We adore our readers and love connecting with them socially.

Like BookSumo on Facebook and let's get social!

Facebook

And also check out the BookSumo Cooking Blog.

Food Lover Blog

Printed in Great Britain
by Amazon